To Gr

MW00699856

THE
GOOD
MANAGER

For Everything

Nov 2020

THE GOOD

MANAGER

Being Great is Overrated!

RALPH PETERSON

Copyright 2020 by Ralph Peterson

All rights reserved. No part of this book may be reproduced, stored in a retrieval system or transmitted, in any form or by any means, without the prior written consent of the publisher, except in the case of brief quotations, embodied in reviews or articles.

Published by Four-Nineteen Press
New York, NY
www.fournineteenpress.com
www.ralphpeterson.com

ISBN: 978-0-9989268-6-5

Photos by Louise Peterson
Book Design: AuthorSupport.com
Proofreading: ProofYourBook.com

10 9 8 7 6 5 4 3 2 1

*"I'm not looking for the best players,
I'm looking for the right ones,"*

Herb Brooks

1980 U.S. Olympic
Hockey Coach

For my grandson Ezra,
who, like his dad
reminds me why it is so
important to always be good.

A SPECIAL THANKS

To Louise, my confidant. For always saying yes when I ask if I can read to you. It takes a special person to sit quietly and listen for months and months, as I ramble on with one idea after another. It isn't easy, and I appreciate you.

CONTENTS

CHAPTER 1

MARCO THE MAGICIAN

I remember jumping up and down with my hands in the air, screaming "Pick me! Pick me!" with all the other kids, when all of a sudden, he did.

"He picked you!" my friend John said pushing me forward.

"Yay!" someone shouted, patting me on the back. "He picked you! He picked you!" Mrs. Clark, the Social Studies teacher made her way through the screaming kids and grabbed my hand, pulling me toward the stage.

"He picked you," she said. Suddenly, I no longer wanted to be picked and I pulled back a little.

"Don't be scared," she said. "It will be fun." She pulled harder. Reluctantly, I followed her to the front of the auditorium and up the stairs to the stage to meet Marco the Magician. I have never been so scared and so excited at that same time.

Marco the Magician walked over and stuck out his hand. I stuck out mine, thinking we were going to shake, but just before we did, an explosion went off and there was a cloud of smoke between us.

"Whoa," Marco said, pulling away from me. "Just my luck. Of all the kids, I picked the one who already knows magic." The kids in the auditorium went crazy. I didn't know what was going on. I just stood there, amazed.

"Don't be shy," Marco said pulling me to the center of the stage. "What is your name?"

"Ralph," I said.

"Okay, Ralph. Do you like bunnies?"

I shrugged.

"I guess so."

"Of course you do," Marco said. "Everyone likes bunnies. Now, I'm going to give you a red ball and a black ball," he said, holding them up for everyone to see. They were about the size of a quarter and made of foam.

I put out both hands, but he waved them away.

"You're only going to need one hand for this trick," he said and placed both of the foam balls into my right hand. Then he had me make a fist.

"Now, tell me Ralph, do you know what happens when you put two bunnies together," he said. I laughed and could feel my ears start to burn with embarrassment. I nodded.

"Speak up," he said while putting the microphone closer to my mouth.

"They have babies," I said, and the kids went wild. Marco backed away, exasperated and Mrs. Clark and all the other teachers in the room looked horrified.

Marco looked at the crowed, then back to me, then back to the crowed. He shook his head in disbelief as if he had heard it all now.

"Oh, no," Marco said laughing. "Well, let's see what happened. Now hold your hand out like this." He made a fist and turned it palm side up. "I'm going to count to three, and when I do, I want you to open your hand."

"One... Two...," all the kids joined in and yelled, "Three!"

I opened my hand and about a million tiny red and black foam bunnies sprang out in all directions. I jumped back and then ran off the stage.

"Give him a hand," Marco said as if my exit was planned. Everyone jumped up and clapped and laughed and gave me high fives as I went back to my seat.

Five years later, I got my first job working as a busboy in a local restaurant called the Steak House. In addition to being known for having the "Juiciest Steak, in New England"–which was their tag line–every Wednesday night they featured none other than... Marco the Magician.

I was in high school at the time, so I only worked Fridays, Saturdays, and Sundays, but evidence of Marco the magician and all the fun he brought to the restaurant was everywhere.

There were playing cards with people's signatures on them, stuck to the ceiling. There were pictures of Marco performing magic tricks to guests at their tables, and there was a whole glass cabinet full of magic tricks and t-shirts and autographed pictures of Marco.

It didn't take long before I told everyone the story about Marco coming to my middle school when I was in the 6th grade and about the bunnies. Everyone loved the story, including, it turned out, Marco.

"Marco wants to know if you can work on Wednesday nights," my boss said.

"Okay," I said, thinking there was no way my Mom would say no, if she knew Marco was asking. I was right. She was just as excited as I was.

Almost immediately, Marco took a liking to me and began to show me some magic tricks. At first, he showed me a couple of card tricks and how to make salt disappear. Then, one night he came in and asked if I wanted to be part of his act.

I remember shaking my head from side to side and backing up

as if to get away from the question. "No, no..." I said. "I would never be as great as you."

"Good," he said with a smile. "Being great is overrated. I just want to you to be really good. Now, c'mon, let me show you." And he did.

CHAPTER 2

THE WARNING

The purpose of any management book, or leadership book for those who prefer to use that vernacular, is to help people become better managers. This help usually comes in the form of "lessons learned" from authors who have spent a considerable amount of time in a management position and have uncovered some helpful information that they want to share with the masses.

This book is similar in the sense that I, too, have spent a considerable amount of time as a manager; and I, too, have learned some valuable lessons along the way. However, this book was not originally written for you, the masses. This book was written for my own management team, and rather than writing another book on management, of which there are plenty to choose from, this book is written as a warning.

First, the good news.

Anyone who is interested in becoming a manager, or a supervisor of any kind, can do so very easily. It doesn't matter what industry you are in, your educational level, your age, gender, and in some cases, even your experience level. If you are willing to raise your hand and declare that you are interested in having more responsibility, (i.e., becoming a manager), someone is always hiring.

However, the number one reason why it is so easy to get promoted into a management position is because there are so many openings. The question you need to be asking yourself is, why.

Why are there so many open positions in management?

Here's the bad news.

The reason there are so many open management positions is because most people do not have what it takes to be a good manager. Worse, those that do have what it takes, are often untrained, unprepared, and have no idea what it means to be a good manager.

To further make the point, consider this: On average, more than five million people are promoted to management positions every year and, on average, more than three million of them will fail within the first ninety days.

That is, two-thirds (or seven out of ten) of all employees who raise their hands and say, "Pick me" will regret making that decision before they have had time to hang family photos on the walls of their new offices.

For those of us in charge of recruiting, promoting, and training managers, the consequences are just as bad. Imagine being in a position where you need to promote one of your best workers into a management position; knowing that, if they fail, you will have to either let them go, or demote them back to their original position. Neither of these options are ideal and worse, you will never know which decision is best until you pick one.

The question, then, is this: Why do so many people get it wrong? And, perhaps more importantly, what can we do about it?

These questions are at the heart of this book and are what I am attempting to answer. But again, as you read this book, keep in mind that it wasn't originally written for the masses; it was written for my own management team, and it is a warning. Take heed.

CHAPTER 3

A Good Manager

"What is a Good Manager," I ask all interviewees. It isn't one of the most interesting questions I have ever asked when interviewing someone for a management position, but the answers always are.

It doesn't matter if I am interviewing a super-worker and they are applying for their first management position or if I am interviewing someone with a lot of management experience I always get the same response to this question.

"A good manager is someone who is a good person," they say.

They are, of course, right. A good manager is someone who is a good person. In fact, one can make a pretty good argument that bad people don't make good managers. But I am looking for a little bit more of an answer to the question, and so I press on, asking for specifics.

Most of the time I will get idealistic words and phrases in return:

"A good manager is someone who is kind and compassionate, someone who helps out, someone who is fair...," and on and on they say.

True. True. True... I nod along.

Sometimes, when I am lucky, I will get someone who answers the question with a question.

"What do you mean by "Good," they say, and it makes me sit up and smile every time. There is more than just a simple dichotomy of the word good; more than just two meanings. In fact, in management, there are three.

First, a good manager is, indeed, a good person. The type of person you want to work for. They don't just set the standards; they live up to them. They are so good, in fact, that if you were to look up the word "good" in the dictionary, you wouldn't be surprised if their smiling face was pictured next to the word.

To be clear, being a good person does not give you the ability to be a good manager. However, it is extremely challenging for anyone to be good at managing if they are not a good person.

People don't like working for people they don't like.

Second, a good manager is also someone who is "good" at managing. Managing is a skill like any other. Sure, some people are naturally good at it and some are not. Either way, being good at managing is a learnable skill.

The challenge with learning how to be good at managing is that it takes more than just time, practice, and education; being good at managing will require you to fundamentally challenge everything you think you know about what it takes to be good.

Finally, there is one more definition, or side to what it means to be a good manager. It is this: A good manager recognizes their proclivity to be evil and they work hard not to be.

I wish I had the ability to fill the space between the end of the last sentence and the beginning of this one with a time delay. I wish I could leave you with that final thought for a while, to make you think about it before you shake your head in disbelief and either dismiss it entirely or ask me to explain. Perhaps the length of this paragraph has been enough. If not, let me say it again:

A good manager recognizes their proclivity to be evil and they work hard not to be.

One of the biggest challenges I continue to face as a manager is matching the appropriate level of punishment to the offense the employee has committed. I cannot tell you how many times I have wanted to overreact to an employee's behavior, even for the smallest infractions against the rules.

Heck, I can't even tell you how many employees I have over-reacted to; there are too many to count.

My point is this: It is very easy to overreact when you are in a management position. Especially considering the imbalance of power, where the manager has much more than the employee. When you couple this power structure with our natural inclination to inflict more harm than we have received, you will start to understand the idea that being a good manager also means not being evil.

In the end, to be "A Good Manager," you have to be a good person; you have to work hard at being good at managing, and you can't be evil.

CHAPTER 4

THE FIVE RULES OF MANAGEMENT

When Marco the Magician took me under his wing, one of the first things he told me about were the five rules for magicians. These rules, he said, needed to be followed by every magician, or magic wouldn't exist.

- Rule #1 Never be a showoff. The more surprised people are, the better the magic
- Rule #2 Always be prepared. Never attempt magic haphazardly

- Rule #3 Never repeat the same trick twice, for the same audience
- Rule #4 Always leave the audience wanting more
- Rule #5 Never, ever... ever... tell the secrets of magic

"These rules are not complicated," he explained. "But they are the basic building blocks of being a good magician. If any magician fails to follow any of these rules, all of magic would suffer."

When I was a kid, I thought it was really cool that all magicians lived by a secret code; and even cooler that I was in the club. However, I don't think I fully understood what he meant when he said, "all of magic would suffer" if anyone violated the rules, until I started watching Youtube.

Youtube is filled with magicians from all over the world showing how every magic trick is performed. They leave nothing unexplained. I'll admit, at first, I was very excited about it. There are (were) a lot of magic tricks that I wanted to know how to perform, and Youtube provided me with step-by-step instructional videos that made them easy to learn.

However, as a consequence, these videos also took away the "Ah, ha!" moments. The surprise... and indeed, the magic.

It is hard to watch any "Marco" type magician now with a sense of awe and wonder. Instead, you learn he probably cut a hole in the bottom of the box, used nylon fishing line attached to his thumb, and he didn't make the card jump out of the box with some magical power, he merely pulled it out with a string. He no longer performs magic... now it's just tricks. And tricks, are a lot less exciting.

Management, like magic, is also based on a set of rules. Rules that need to be followed by every manager, or the entire profession of management suffers.

- Rule #1 Managers are not allowed to walk by trash
- Rule #2 Managers must always be on time
- Rule #3 Managers must dress professionally
- Rule #4 Managers must be good workers
- Rule #5 Managers must be visible

Like magic, these rules are not complicated; they are basic. In fact, they are so basic, that many managers view them as mere suggestions, while others disregard them completely.

I wish I could be crass about these managers. I wish I could say that I don't care, that it doesn't matter to me if they fail. However, I am forced to care. The truth is, like magic, when a manager breaks any of the rules of management, all of management suffers.

CHAPTER 5

Rule #1
Managers Are Not Allowed to Walk by Trash

The first rule in management is also the easiest to understand: "Managers are not allowed to walk by trash." As you can see, you do not need an advanced degree or some specialized training to understand the intent of this rule, or its importance. In fact, if you have ever been promoted to a leadership position, it is quite possible that you are already the type of person who doesn't walk by trash. Indeed, it is probably one of the main reasons why you were promoted in the first place.

Unfortunately, just because something is easy to understand, doesn't mean it is easy to do. Or, to put it another way, because let's be honest, not walking by trash is as easy to do as it is to understand, let me say it this way: I know, when something is easy to do, it is just as easy not to do. Here in, lies the problem and the need for rule #1. Managers are not allowed to walk by trash.

Trash, of course, is simply a metaphor for anything that is out of place and easily correctable. Other examples are things like unsecured doors that are supposed to be locked, or equipment and supplies not put away properly. In these cases, rule #1 would read: Managers are not allowed to walk by unsecured doors or equipment and supplies that are not put away properly.

Again, keep in mind that this book was not written for you, the masses, but for my management team specifically. Also, please remember that this book is written as a warning. So, to my management team, let me say this:

WARNING: If you walk trash and I see you do it, I will write you up. If I write you up three times, I will let you go.

By the way, as a little side bar to "letting someone go." Keep in mind that this is the best turn-of-phrase to use when firing someone. If you can help it, never use the word "fire" unless you intend to sit around one with a few friends and a bag of marshmallows.

Other phrases like, "We are going to make today your last day," or "We are going to leave it here..." are also better. They are certainly a lot less hostile and more professional than, "You're fired!"

Trust me; and don't walk by trash.

CHAPTER 6

RULE #2
MANAGERS MUST ALWAYS BE ON TIME

The second rule for managers is a tough one. The rule is: Managers must always be on time. You wouldn't think this would be a tough rule to follow, but it is. There are two main reasons why this rule is so difficult for managers.

The first reason is because most managers either get to choose what time they start work and/or there isn't anyone above them making sure they start on time. The reason for this is because managers are trusted to always "do the right thing," especially when it comes to something as easy as being at work on time.

The second reason why managers struggle with this rule is because of what I call the "unspoken benefits rule" that all managers assume, but are never given.

Let's begin with the first one.

If I have seen it once, I have seen it a hundred times, if a manager is allowed to choose when they start their day, most of them will choose the time they show up, as the time they are "supposed to" show up. Meaning, there is no consistency. Today they might show up at 7:30am, and tomorrow it might be closer to 7:45am. The day after that, they may not show up until 9am.

Anyone who dares to question them will be met with a stern look and a terse phrase reminding them who asks who the questions.

"Do you know who I am?" Imagine I am shaking my head side-to-side and my tone is riddled with sarcasm.

If you have the ability to choose what time you start each day, do yourself and your team a favor and choose. If it is 7am, then make it 7am. If it is 8am, then make it 8am. Whatever time makes the most sense for your business (notice I did not say whatever time is most convenient for you), choose that time and communicate it with your staff. Let everyone know what time they can expect you every day. Don't give them a time frame (don't say, "I'll be in sometime between 7 and 10"); give an actual time and then do everything you can to not be late.

The second reason why this rule is so difficult for some managers, especially new managers, is two-fold. First, it is because of what the new manager believes and second, it's because of what their spouse, life partner, parents, kids, relatives, and friends believe; it is the same thing, and it is wrong.

I am talking about the unspoken benefits rule.

I want to say that this only affects new managers, but I know better. I have worked with a lot of people who have been managing for years and years, who believe in the unspoken benefits rule.

The unspoken benefits rule is this: As part of the management salary package, most people believe when they get promoted to management, they also get an additional benefit of being allowed to come and go as they please.

They believe managers have the right to come in late and leave early. They believe they should get more breaks, take longer lunches and some even believe they can take time during the working day to run personal errands.

The challenge for many managers is, even if they do not believe in the unspoken benefits rule, I guarantee there are people in their life (their spouse, kids, parents, etc.) that do. They will use it against the manager to force them to take extra time in the morning, which makes them late or puts pressure on them to run an errand during the day or leave early.

"You are in charge now!" They say. "You can be late. You can leave early. You can skip out for a bit. No one is going to say anything to you!"

They are right, of course. Most employees won't speak up, but they will all notice, and they will judge you harshly for it, because it isn't fair. Do it too many times and you will go from having the potential to be a good manager, to a statistical anomaly, like so many others before you.

WARNING: As with all rules, if one of my managers is late, I will write them up. If a manager is late three times, I will let them go.

Managers, to be good, you have to be on time. There are no acceptable excuses.

CHAPTER 7

Rule #3
Managers Must Dress Professionally

The third rule for managers is: Managers must dress professionally. However, this rule could be modified to read, "Managers must dress so that they stand out." That is, managers need be recognizable from a distance or in a crowd of employees. Sometimes it means a business suit, and other times it might mean a different colored hard hat or lab coat. In either case, managers must always do their best to look professional and stand out.

This, again, sounds like a simple enough rule for managers to adhere to. However, I cannot tell you how many times I have had to talk to managers about dressing appropriately and professionally. Everywhere I look, managers are dressing like their staff, seemingly unwilling to dress better and stand out. It wasn't until I saw a documentary on zebras, of all things, that I finally figured out why.

If you have ever seen a zebra, you know it has a unique black and white striped color pattern. It turns out, researchers have been trying to figure out why zebras have black and white stripes, especially since nothing in the zebras' natural environment is black and white. Meaning, if you look at nearly any other animal in the wild, you will see that they all do a pretty good job blending in with their environment except zebras.

Then, quite accidentally, a group of researchers believed they may have stumbled upon the answer. While attempting to understand the migration patterns of a group of zebras, the researchers decided to capture and tag a few of them with a tracking device that included large yellow tags, which they attached to their ear.

While waiting to track the zebras' migration, a terrible and unexpected thing happened to every single zebra that had a yellow tracking device tag; they were eaten by a lion.

Not good.

It turns out, the black and white stripes on a zebra help them to blend together as a group. When a lion or other predator sees a pack of zebras, it is hard for them to distinguish one zebra from another, or where one begins and one ends, due to their black and white stripes. However, as soon as the researchers put a large yellow tag in the ear of a few of them, the lions were able to pick them out easily.

"Ah, ha!" I said, getting up and pausing the television. "That is why managers do not like to stand out; they are afraid of the lions."

Of course, in this case, the "lions" are unhappy customers, or employees. And, just like lions, if something goes wrong and the customer or the employee needs to complain to someone, who do they look for? They look for the person who stands out. They look for the person who looks like they are in charge, and then, they attack.

Here's the thing: Zebras, and anyone else who doesn't want to stand out in a crowd, do not make good managers. To be a good manager, you have to be more like a lion, or at the very least, you can't be afraid of them.

I would add that there is another reason why it is important for managers to dress professionally; it is because managing is not only about problem solving, it is also about influencing. Getting people to follow your lead.

Behavioral researchers from Texas conducted a handful of studies to find out if the way someone looks makes a difference when trying to influence others. It does.

My favorite experiment they conducted was with a guy in his mid-thirties. Dressed in jeans and a T-shirt, they had him jaywalk across a busy intersection before the light changed, and then counted the number of people who followed him across. It wasn't very many.

Then, they dressed the same guy in a business suit and again, had him jaywalk across a busy intersection before the light changed. This time, the number of people who followed the guy in the business suit was nearly four times as many.

It turns out, more people are willing to follow someone who is dressed professionally, even if, by following them, they are actually breaking the law.

Rule number three cannot be overstated. Dressing professionally and standing out are vital to being a good manager.

WARNING: As always, if one of my managers does not dress professionally, or if they try to blend in rather than trying to stand out, I will write them up. If I write them up three times, I will let them go.

CHAPTER 8

Rule #4
Managers Must Get Their Work Done

Any time I need a new manager, the first thing I do is look at all of my best workers, hoping to find the diamond in the rough. When I say the best, of course, I mean the best of the best; the "Super-Worker." The type of worker that is always on time. They always get their work done. They are smart and resourceful, and they are always willing to help out.

These are the types of workers who make the best managers.

It is not foolproof, of course and I can't tell you how many people love to point that out to me, "You know, just because so and so is a good worker, doesn't mean they will be a good manager," they say.

"I know... I know..." I say, trying hard not to roll my eyes.

It is as if they think I have a choice. I don't. Could you imagine if I tried to promote the worst workers into management positions? My employees would think I have gone mad. Think about it.

We have all worked with someone that wasn't a good worker. The type of person who is always late and never gets their work done on time. The type of person who spends more time and energy coming up with ways not to work than they do actually working.

Now, imagine that person getting promoted into a management position, and now they are your boss. How would that make you feel?

I'll tell you how it makes me feel and it is not good. It makes me feel like the whole universe just started spinning backwards; up is down, down is up, and there must be something going on between the hiring manager and that girl (wink, wink...), because there is no way she should have been promoted to management.

On the flip side, something bad happens to a lot of "super-workers" who get promoted into management positions: they go from always getting their work done to struggling to get anything done, which of course, is a direct violation to rule number four and the main reason why so many people are quick to point out how this strategy isn't foolproof.

Rule #4: Managers must get all of their work done on time.

For many years, I believed managers struggled to get their work done on time because of an attitude problem that is prevalent among new managers. Unfortunately, many new managers treat their promotion into management like they just won the lottery and they will never have to work again. Getting over this feeling of superiority can be quite challenging.

However, after many years and hundreds of promotions and training new managers, I have come to realize that, although this attitude problem is a real thing that needs to be addressed, it is not the complete story. In fact, many mangers simply don't know how to both manage and get their own work done. Learning how to do both takes a lot of training, a lot of skill, and a lot of experience; none of which new managers have.

Two of the most common reasons why most managers struggle to get their work done, are time management and, to a greater extent, an open-door policy.

First, time management or, what I like to call, the freshman fifteen.

The "freshman fifteen" is a turn-of-phrase that denotes a common occurrence among first-time college students; they gain weight. Although there are numerous studies that have turned up all kinds of reasons why this occurs, every one of them agree on one thing: Eighteen year olds, given the freedom and flexibility away from their parents for the first time, will over-do... well, everything, including eating. Therefore, it is very common for first year college students to gain weight (on average, fifteen pounds).

This same thing happens to new managers. As soon as a new manager gets a taste of freedom and flexibility, because no one is looking over their shoulder, they lose sight of the clock and spend time as if they have a ton to spare. Soon, they are taking longer breaks, having more in-depth conversations with co-workers about nothing, spending more time in their offices, usually scrolling through social media on their phone and, in the end, getting a lot less work done.

Soon, the end of the day arrives and the new manager tries to make a last ditch effort to cram a full days' worth of work into the last sixty minutes, only to realize, thirty minutes in that there is no way they are going to be able to finish on time.

So, what do they do? They either try to put it off to the next day, or worse, they end up taking their work home; vowing to finish their work between making dinner and doing laundry or during commercial breaks while watching their favorite television show. In either case, the outcome is not good.

Having an open-door policy, however, is even worse.

In theory, an open-door policy makes sense. You may even think it is the right kind of policy to have. It is a feel-good policy that encourages all of your staff members to feel free to come to you directly for any and all assistance.

You think you are doing the right thing, but you are not.

There are a few reasons why an open-door policy isn't the best management practice. Things like, it promotes reactive rather than proactive management and only those who have the time and ability to come to you get help. However, the number one reason why you should not have an open door-policy is because of what researchers call "the interruption principle."

Simply put, the interruption principle is this: On average, it takes people nearly 25 minutes to refocus on a task after they have been interrupted.

Now, I don't know about you, but if I let people "pop in" on me whenever they wanted, I would be interrupted at least ten times a day, which translates into more than four hours of lost time. No wonder managers can't get their work done on time.

Close the door.

The best thing managers can do is replace their open-door policy with two things: First, have office hours posted, so that if someone does need to see you they can schedule time to meet with you.

Second, leave your office and start managing by walking around... in short, be visible (but we will get to that rule, next).

WARNING: If any of my managers do not get their work done on time, I will write them up. If I write them up three times, I will let them go.

CHAPTER 9

RULE #5
MANAGERS MUST BE VISIBLE

learned it intuitively, long before I was old enough to drive, that any time you see a "No U-Turn" sign on the highway you are supposed to take your foot off the gas and slow down; there might be a police officer there.

If there is, simply check your speed, slow down and obey the laws. Move into the right lane and put your hands at ten and two. If not, feel free to hammer back down on the gas pedal and keep going; the laws be damned.

A few years ago, I was hosting a leadership workshop for a police department. At the time, a new type of GPS navigational software had just come out called WAZE. The unique thing about this app, was two-fold: One, the GPS would show you the fastest way to get to your destination, and two, users could report potential hazards right on the app, which is pretty cool. This included everything from construction zones to broken down cars, and even potholes and animals. However, the coolest thing about the app is it allows users to tell each other where the police are.

Suddenly, you no longer had to look for those U-Turn signs; using the WAZE app, you can now see and report where all the police are. I asked the officers in the workshop how this new app affected their job.

"I use it to check in," a police officer in the back of the room said and laughed.

I remember shaking my head from side to side, a big smile on my face because it seemed funny. Not really "ha ha" funny, but weird funny. I asked him to clarify the best way I knew how.

"Huh?" I said.

He explained that, ever since everyone started using the WAZE app, more people knew where he was and less people sped by him.

"That gave me an idea," he said with a grin, not sure if he should be saying this out loud to the group of officers.

"So, I started using it to check in," he said scanning the room. No one seemed to know what he was talking about. I waved at him with my hand, letting him know that I, too, needed more details.

"Normally, before the new app," he said, almost dismissively. "I would try my best to hide my car off the side of the highway, in the woods so that no one could see me.

"Now, with the new WAZE app, people identify me and tag me on the app before I even get turned around. It is no longer helpful to try to hide. As soon as one person sees you, everyone gets notified where you are.

"So now, not only do I not try to hide my cruiser, but I just pull the app up on my phone and check in myself." He picked up his cell phone off the desk and pretended the app was open. "I'm right here," he said tapping his finger on the screen.

"Then I sit back and enjoy my coffee." He laughed. It took a minute, but eventually, everyone in the room started to understand the genius of this move and they all began to laugh with him. A couple of officers even clapped.

Me, I sat on the edge of the desk and shook my head in disbelief. "Holy cow," I murmured. "H.O.L.Y. freakin' cow."

What that officer reminded me of, heck, what he reminded all of us of, is if you are in any type of leadership position, being visible has a profound effect on everyone around you. If you know a police officer is around the corner, you will check your speed. Your hands find their way to ten and two, like they are supposed to, and you do everything right, as you drive by.

The same thing happens when employees know their manager is present and always walking around.

This brings me to Rule #5 Managers must always be visible

WARNING: If I find that one of my managers is not being visible, I will write them up. If I write them up three times, I will let them go.

CHAPTER 10

FOLLOWING THE RULES ISN'T ENOUGH

Research shows that, to be effective, rules do not need to be overly complicated. In fact, the more basic the rules are, the more likely they will be understood, remembered, and followed.

The five rules for managers are not complicated; they are, indeed, basic. However, you should not mistake the word basic for easy. These rules may sound easy but trust me, they are not. Or, to reiterate the dichotomy of the term, easy: "Anything that is easy to do, is just as easy not to do." If you add in a hint of authority and mix it with just the right amount of freedom, you will find that following these "easy" rules, becomes a lot less "easy;" especially for managers.

The truth is, if a person has the ability to choose between following the rules or not following the rules, most will choose the latter. It doesn't matter if you are an employee or a manager. I am speaking from experience here. If given the opportunity to cut corners, especially if it is likely that I will not get caught, or get in trouble for doing so you can bet money I will cut corners. In the end, I am just like everyone else: human.

That is not to say that all humans cut corners; but it is to say that I needed someone looking over my shoulder when I was an employee and when I was a front line manager, and more than likely, so do you. Hence, the reason I end every rule with the same warning:

WARNING: "If, I find one of my managers not following any of the rules of management, I will write them up. If I write them up three times, I will let them go."

And I mean it.

These rules, as basic as they seem, are the foundation of effective management. You cannot effectively manage people, and be able to hold them accountable for being on time, if you are not consistently on time.

You cannot effectively manage people, and hold them accountable for dressing appropriately, if you do not dress appropriately.

You cannot effectively manage people, and hold them accountable for getting all of their work done on time, if you do not get your work done on time. Your employees need to see you just as busy as you expect them to be.

Finally, you cannot effectively manage people if you spend all of your time sitting in your office, shopping on Amazon, scrolling on Facebook or, God forbid, playing Candy Crush while waiting for people to bring their problems to you, under some false pretense that having an open door policy is enough. It isn't. To be effective, you have to be on your feet and walking around. That is, you have to be visible.

These rules are the backbone of effective management. And the most important thing about them is what they say about you, the manager. In short, they help you answer the question that everyone is asking: Why are you in charge. Why should anyone listen to you. Why should anyone follow you. Your title (the manager) will only take you so far.

Your actions will take you everywhere.

In contrast, simply following these rules will not make you a good manager. In fact, everyone should be expected to follow these rules; employees, leads, assistants, supervisors, managers, and even CEO's and presidents. Following these rules are what makes you a good employee.

To be a good manager, however, following these rules are not enough; the secret is, to be a good manager, you have to be able to get others to follow these rules. Now that is managing.

Case in point: Rule #1 says, "Managers are not allowed to walk by trash." However, to be a good manager, not only should managers not walk by trash, but they should also not pick it up.

Once again, I wish I had the ability to make you pause here. To give you time to think about that last sentence before you move on. I don't. So instead, let me say it again:

Rule #1 "Managers are not allowed to walk by trash AND they are not allowed to pick it up."

Here is the million-dollar question: If you are not allowed to walk by trash and you are not allowed to pick it up, then what are you supposed to do? Stand by every piece of trash until it's time to go home? Wait for the person who dropped the trash to come back and pick it up? Or maybe, you should wait for the housekeeping department to come by?

No. No. No.

A good manager does not walk by trash and they do not pick it up. Instead they get someone else to pick it up. That is, they manage.

CHAPTER 11

THE BLACK SWAN

Have you ever seen a black swan?

If you are like most people, not only have you never seen a black swan, you have probably never considered whether or not there is such a thing. There is.

However, there was a time when all of society believed that only white swans existed. In fact, the term "white swan" was used as a common idiom, or an expression that denoted a metaphorical meaning. Consider the phrase: "piece of cake," or "break a leg," or, it "takes two to tango..."

There was a time when phrases like these also included a reference to white swans: Imagine something being, "as white as a swan," or as pure... The reason this phrase was so popular is because, at the time, no one had ever seen anything other than white swans. In fact, no one believed swans came in any other color–except white. Until 1697 that is, when a Dutch explorer discovered black swans in Western Australia and brought them back to Europe.

It may seem silly now, but the discovery of the black swan shook the modern Europeans to their core. In a society that believed they were governed by a set of undeniable (and unchangeable) truths by God, the discovery of the black swan forced them to question everything. Keep in mind, this is the same society that, nearly a century before, burned a catholic priest alive because he dared to say that the sun, and not the earth, was at the center of the universe.

To say the discovery of the black swans took everyone by surprise, would be an understatement. Suddenly, everyone began to question everything.

Ever since it's discovery, the Black Swan has been used as a metaphor, or proof, that not everything is as it seems. There are, indeed, more ways to skin a cat, (to use another common idiom), or, a different side to every story.

The same is true in management.

I remember when I first became interested in management. I used to watch everything my manager did with a skeptical eye. In truth, I thought he was an idiot. I thought he had no idea what he was doing and, of course, I thought I would be a much better manager than he was. In fact, I thought I was going to be the greatest manager of all time.

Then, I became a manager and, to my utter dismay, it turned out, I didn't know the first thing about managing. Worse, all of my pie in the sky, idealistic beliefs about what it took to be a great manager were more than just misguided; they were wrong.

I used to believethat, to be a great manager, all you had to do was set the example and everyone would follow your lead. That was, until I was pulled aside by another manager who asked why I was always picking up trash.

"I'm leading by example," I said with a condescending tone. He laughed.

"Right," he said. "You know, you are the only one picking up trash, don't you?" I opened my mouth to protest, but before I could, he pointed at my hands. "You are literally walking around with a broom and dustpan." I could feel my ears burn with embarrassment. He was right. I don't know when it started, but at some point, I got tired of constantly bending over to pick up trash, so I started walking around with a broom and one of those dustpans on a stick.

I felt like a fool and apparently, I looked like one too.

"That's not your job," he said. "It's theirs," he gestured to a group of employees pretending to be busy. "Your job is to make sure they do it."

If you would have asked me why I was always the one picking

up trash, as the manager, I would have told you something that I sincerely believed.

"You can't expect someone to do something that you are not willing to do yourself." At the time not only did I believe it, but if I am being honest, it was a belief that I hid behind.

I know what you are thinking; How does someone believe in something and hide behind it at the same time? It turns out, it's pretty easy; I wanted it to be true, even though all the evidence suggested it wasn't.

The truth is, I have never been so good at picking up trash, that I got it all. Every time I walked out of my office, there was always more trash on the floor. It didn't matter if I had just walked around and picked it all up or if it had been hours. Trash seemed to appear out of thin air like magic.

It took me a long time to figure out what to do, and then it took me even longer to do it. Not only because it was hard (and trust me when I say it was hard, it is) but because it went against everything I was ever taught (and believed) about what it took to be a good person, and more importantly, a good manager.

In fact, I believed in all the "Golden Rules" my parents taught me. In addition to believing that you should never ask anyone to do something that you would not do, I was also raised to believe that managers should: treat people the way they want to be treated, should always praise publicly and reprimand privately, should always choose their battles, and, that micro-managing, of course, was bad. A good manager shouldn't have to check in on their staff all the time.

Heck, while I'm being honest, I should tell you, I even believed that managers were entitled to special favors and privileges and, don't laugh, though it seems ridiculous to me now I thought all of this "management stuff," was going to be easy.

However, just like the Europeans seeing a black swan for the first time, I eventually had to face the truth. Everything I thought I knew about management; indeed, everything I was taught about what it takes to be a good manager, was wrong.

CHAPTER 12

THE GOLDEN RULES OF LEADERSHIP

In 2018, Ohio State University suspended their head football coach, Urban Meyer, for three games to include the university's first home game when they learned that one of his assistant managers had multiple allegations of domestic abuse.

To be clear: No one made any allegations of any type of abuse against the head coach. In fact, Coach Meyer didn't do anything to cover up the allegations, or try to downplay the seriousness of the charges.

He did the opposite.

As soon as Coach Meyer learned of the allegations against the assistant coach (Zach Smith), he called a press conference and told them everything he knew about the situation, including the actions he took against the assistant coach which included an immediate suspension, pending an investigation.

However, after an exhausting 11-hour meeting, the board of trustees decided to suspend the head coach and the athletic director, without pay, for their actions in this case.

When asked why the board thought suspending the head coach over the (suspected) actions of one of his assistant coaches, especially in light of Coach Meyer's actions (i.e. suspending the assistant coach and going public with the decision) the board responded: '...that even though Coach Meyer did not:'

"...condone or cover up the alleged domestic abuse by Zach Smith, {he} failed to take sufficient management action..."

Think about that for a minute. What did the board expect the coach to do? What would you have done in a situation like this? What does "sufficient management action," mean exactly?

By all accounts, Coach Meyer seemed to be trying to do the right thing. However, when asked what he thought about the board's decision, he agreed with them, saying:

"I followed my heart and not my head."

See, what Coach Meyer was following, the ideas and principles he based all of his management decision on, are what we call the "Golden Rules" of management.

1. Praise publicly and reprimand privately
2. Never ask anyone to do something you wouldn't do
3. Choose your battles
4. Never micromanage your team
5. Treat people the way you want to be treated

These are the ideas and principles (the Golden Rules) that led to Coach Meyer's decision and ultimately, what got him trouble. He followed his heart instead of his head.

The board of directors believed the only acceptable, "sufficient management action" would have been to fire the assistant coach.

For a long time, I would have cried foul if I were told that the right thing to do is fire someone over allegations. I mean, if no one was convicted of anything, then how can you fire them?

However, the board was right.

Being in charge is more than just being responsible for the outcomes of your team's products and services. It is more than simply making sure your employees clock in and out on time, or that they have enough supplies and they get their holiday pay.

Managers are role models, and not only for your employees, but for your company. As a manager, you represent everyone. This means, whatever you do, it affects them.

You cannot be a good manager and be arrested for allegations of drinking and driving, or stealing, or domestic abuse even if you haven't gone to court and "officially" been convicted of anything. Simply being charged with a crime is bad enough.

I wish I could tell you the "Golden Rules" of management are true. Heck, I wish they were true. I wish we could all follow our hearts and be good managers. Unfortunately, we can't. Trust me, I have believed in, and followed every one of these rules and I have suffered because of it.

I have been fired, let go, demoted, punished, ridiculed, reprimanded, reassigned, embarrassed, provoked, called foolish, ineffective, and worst of all disgruntled. And the whole time, I thought the problem was them... It wasn't. It was me.

Me, wanting to feel good rather than being effective. Me, hiding behind my principles. Me, not wanting to take a stand. Me, being embarrassed. Me, being scared. Me, and my misunderstanding of what it takes to be a good manager. Me, believing in some arbitrary set of rules, that honestly could have been written by a group of employees who used feel-good tactics to disarm managers and enable them to do less and less. It was all me.

CHAPTER 13

Golden Rule #1
Praise Publicly &
Reprimand Privately

I grew up watching television shows like Superman, Mighty Mouse, Casper the Friendly Ghost, Scooby Doo, the Dukes of Hazard, and Happy Days. All of these TV shows had one thing in common they were all based on the scenario of good guys vs. bad guys.

I always wanted to be a good guy.

In fact, I always thought I was one of the good guys. It is one of the main things that attracted me to management at such an early age; I always wanted to be a hero.

And, truth be told, it looked easy. Someone gets in trouble. They don't know where to turn. Everything seems helpless and dire until... cue superhero music... a hero comes flying in, or rolling up on a motorcycle. Sometimes they even get to wear capes, and they always save the day.

That's me. Or, at least, I wanted that to be me.

As a hero, I always knew my job was to do the right thing. However, I would come to learn that "knowing" what the right thing to do is not as easy as they made it look on television.

The first time I had to reprimand someone, it was for being late which you wouldn't think would be all that hard, but it was. I remember calling the employee into my office, shutting the door, and fiddling with a bunch of papers on my desk before I finally got the courage to start the conversation; when I did, I talked in a whisper.

I didn't do this to reprimand him privately, to save him the embarrassment of being called into the manager's office, I did it because I was embarrassed. Heck, I was more than just embarrassed, I was scared. It was my first time having to have a difficult conversation with someone and I was the one who needed privacy.

It wasn't long before I was having difficult conversations with people for all kinds of reasons and my office became more than a quiet room, it became my safe place. It was set up perfectly. My desk, which faced the door, was large, made of wood, and kept me and the person I was reprimanding at least four feet apart. This gave me the confidence I needed to say whatever I needed to say. I even had a name plate on my desk that let everyone know I was in charge: "Ralph Peterson, Manager" it read.

At the time, if you would have asked me why I had difficult conversations in my office, I would have told you I did it for them. That I believed, if you had to reprimand someone, and you wanted to be a good manager, you should do it privately.

It felt good to be that kind of a manager. The idea that even if you do something wrong, I was still going to be the type of person who doesn't embarrass you in front of others; that I was still going to be a good manager.

However, being good is not the same as being good at it. And from a management point of view, this policy of mine, was short-sighted and caused more problems than it solved.

I remember the day I found this out like it was yesterday. I had an employee, a young guy who referred to himself as Triple D, because his first, middle and last name all started with the letter D.

He was 18 or 19 years old, had an attitude problem, told everyone he was going to be a famous singer, and had a terrible attendance record. He called out more days than he worked. When he did show up for work, he was always late, asked to leave early, and did a horrible job.

After dealing with him for a few weeks, I finally brought him into my office and told him I had enough. That I was taking him off the schedule. He immediately started to protest. "Triple D, this and Triple D, that..." He said begging me to keep him on the schedule.

I let him grovel for a few minutes before I finally agreed to give him one more chance. "No more being late, or trying to leave early, and you have to get all of your work done," I said. He agreed. "And," I said pulling out a piece of paper, "You have to sign this." I handed him an employee warning notice that I had already filled out.

He stared at me hard for a minute, but I just stared back as expressionless as possible. I shrugged and held it out further.

"Okay," he said. "Okay." He took the write up and signed it.

Fifteen minutes later, I was on my way into the employee break room to heat up my lunch when I overheard one of the other employees ask him why I wanted to see him in my office. It stopped me in my tracks. I leaned against the concrete wall and strained to listen.

"He didn't want anything," he said.

"Really," another employee snorted in disbelief. None of the other staff members liked him because he was so unreliable.

"Yeah," he said. "He didn't want anything. He just talked to me about some of the work we are doing."

"Unbelievable," the first employee said. I could picture them all in there, eating leftovers and cold sandwiches for lunch and judging me based on what Triple D was saying. They knew he was a terrible employee and now they thought I was a terrible manager.

He was lying, but it didn't matter. They had no way of knowing the truth. They had no idea that I had talked to him a bunch of times. That I had written him up twice and that I had just threatened to let him go if he didn't start showing up and working. They had no idea, because I was too busy hiding in my office and telling myself that I was doing the right thing by not embarrassing anyone.

That's the rub. If you want to be a good person–then go ahead, close the door and do everything in private. However, if you want to be a good manager, you need to avoid closed office spaces and hushed tones. You need to speak up just loud enough and public enough for everyone to see that you are managing everyone the same; that you are, indeed, a good manager.

Over the years, I have learned how to reprimand publicly without making a big spectacle of it. If someone is late, for instance, I will wait for them in the hall, looking at my watch when they show up, "We start at 7," I say loud enough for someone to hear me.

I need everyone to know that I don't let things slide.

If I do have to write them up, or if a more private conversation is needed, I will start the conversation in the hall, making sure someone overhears me and then, just before we get into anything too private, I will ask the employee to come with me to my office.

If I need to write up a manager, I will ask another manager if they have a copy of an Employee Warning Notice.

"Of course," they say nervously. "Who are you writing up?"

"Not you," I say taking the notice. I can always hear their feet as they rush to the door behind me so they can see whose office I go into next.

Indeed, over the years, I have become very good at making sure everyone knows when someone is being reprimanded.

When it comes to praising, the same dichotomy exists. The truth is, most public praising is a good thing. However, it too can backfire.

Here is the truth. You are going to have favorites. There isn't much you can do about it. There are going to be some employees that you get along with a lot better than others. However, if you want to be a good manager, no one can ever know.

At the same time, and more of an aside, than anything else, there are also going to be employees that you don't like. The key to being a good manager is, they too can never know.

In the end, being a hero is a lot tougher than it looks; but it's worth it.

CHAPTER 14

Golden Rule #2
Never Ask Anyone to Do Anything You Wouldn't Do

One of the biggest challenges managers face is feeling worthy.

It doesn't matter if you are new to managing and this is your first time being in charge, or if you have been managing for a long time. Every time someone is put in charge, or when they hire a new team member, managers feel the need to explain or justify why they are the manager.

We see this play out in all kinds of ways. Some managers will tell their new team members all about their education. Others will focus on the amount of time they have in a particular field. Experienced managers will often highlight the number of years they have been managing, and then there are others who will describe in detail their vast experiences; often telling their origin story of how they rose through the ranks to become a manager.

All of this is to say, "I am worthy of being in charge."

However, although this is all well and good and probably necessary for many managers, most employees don't care about where their new manager comes from, how long they have been managing, or where they went to school. Most employees only care about one thing; that is, how is the new manager going to treat them.

No worries. Just as managers feel the need to justify their position of power, they are just as eager to tell the employees what they can expect from them; and guess what... It is all good.

"I have an open-door policy," they explain, assuring everyone that they are approachable. "And I am not a micro-manager," they declare with pride. "I am easygoing." "I am fair." "I believe the company should buy everyone lunch at least once a month," they continue. (I wish I were making that last one up; I'm not).

Then they say the turn-of-phrase that gets most of them in trouble: "I would never ask anyone to do anything I wouldn't do." That's when everyone's eyes get big.

"Oh really," they think. "I can't wait to see that. I can't wait to see the manager come in on their day off to cover a shift, or help unload a truck by hand because the forklift is still broken, or clean the bathrooms... oh, I can't wait to see the manager clean the bathrooms."

Of course, most managers didn't mean it that way. They didn't mean to say that they wouldn't ask anyone to do their job without first proving they would do the job but that is how it is taken by employees. If managers are not careful, that is how they, too, will start viewing their own job; as someone who has to do everything, just to prove to everyone else that they are worthy.

It is an easy trap to fall into.

To highlight how easy it is for managers to fall into this trap, consider what it takes to get promoted into management. First, you have to be really good at your job. In most cases, you have to be really good at a lot of people's jobs. Next, you have to be helpful and curious and dependable. You have to be the type of employee who is willing to do whatever it takes to get the job done even when it is not directly your job. In short, you have to be a super worker.

That's when it happens.

You get recognized for all of your hard work. You get praise for always willing to step up and help out. Soon, you're asked to consider whether you would like more responsibility. You say yes, a promotion is offered and poof, just like that, you are now in charge.

Is it any wonder, then, why so many managers are willing to stand behind the Golden Rule of, "I would never ask anyone to do anything that I wouldn't do?" Of course not. Most managers spend years and years going above and beyond to prove to everyone around them that they are worthy of being in charge. They earned it through hard work, and they think they have to keep earning it, well after they get promoted. The truth is, they don't.

CHAPTER 15

Counter Point: Leadership Capital

"I was raised to believe you should always lead from the front," Jane said. "And now you are telling me not to?" I nodded.

"That's right," I said.

"Why would anyone ever listen to me if I refused to do the things I am asking them to do?" She said as she shook her head from side to side. Absent-mindedly, she started to move papers around on her desk. "It just doesn't seem right."

"I know," I said. "Because you are looking at it wrong." She looked up, smiled, and then leaned back in her chair. She folded her arms across her chest and pointed her chin toward me.

"You tell me then," she said. "What should I do."

"Have you ever heard of something called, 'leadership capital'" I said, using hand quotes. She shook her head no.

"Leadership capital is something you earn, through leading others. It's just like money. It can be earned, it can be saved, and it can even be spent. In fact, it can be given away. And, just like real money, the more you have, the more you can buy." I paused, making eye contact with her to see if she was following me. Her eyes got big and she nodded.

"At the same time, just like money, the more you have, the more power and control you have and the more you can do." She continued to nod cautiously.

"Only, we are not talking about money, we are talking about leadership. Does that make sense?" She squinted and sat up.

"Kind of," she said.

"Let me try to explain it like this," I said. "Have you ever played the board game Monopoly?" She nodded and laughed. "Good," I said. "Then let's play Monopoly." I took out a piece of paper and drew four squares; one in each corner. Then I labeled them to mirror an actual Monopoly board.

On the bottom right square I wrote the word "GO." On the bottom left, I drew a small jail cell in the center of the square and then wrote the words "Just visiting" all around it. On the top left, I wrote "Free Parking," and on the top right I wrote, "GO TO JAIL" in big capital letters.

I spun the paper around so she could see it. She looked at it and then nodded. "Okay," she said. I smiled.

"Okay," I agreed. "What is the goal of Monopoly?"

"To win," she said.

"Thank you," I said, and we both laughed until our stomachs hurt. Finally, I said, "Can you be a bit more specific?"

"To have the most money," she said.

"Ah! Good," I said. "Now tell me, what is the easiest way to make money playing Monopoly?" Jane thought about if for a minute, but hesitated. She thought it was a trick question. It wasn't. I pointed at the square with the word "GO" on it. "What happens every time someone passes "GO?"

"They get $200," she said.

"Right," I said. "So we can agree. The easiest way to make money in Monopoly, is by simply rolling the dice and passing "GO." She nodded.

"Yeah, but it is not that easy," she said pointing toward my hand-written Monopoly board. "You are missing a lot of squares here."

"I know," I said waiving her hand away. "Don't get ahead of me." She laughed and rolled her eyes.

"Stay with me here," I said. "The easiest way to make money playing Monopoly is by rolling the dice and moving your player around the board. Every time you pass "GO" you collect $200." She pursed her lips and nodded.

"Earning leadership capital is the same thing; except, instead of rolling dice, you move ahead by following the Five Rules for managers. The more you follow the Five Rules, the more leadership capital you earn. Make sense?"

Jane sat back and smiled. "Now that you are explaining it like this, it does."

"Good," I said. "So, you can see, the more days, weeks, months, and years, that you follow the Five Rules, the more leadership capital you earn." Jane nodded. "And, the more leadership capital you have, the more you are able to buy. Which, in leadership, means that you will be a more effective manager." Jane's smile grew wider.

"This is really helpful," she said.

"Wait," I said. "I didn't tell you the bad part yet."

"I don't want to hear the bad part," Jane said laughing.

"Too bad," I said. "What do you think, managing is easy?" She laughed and shook her head.

"I know better than that," she said. "It is the hardest thing I have ever done."

"Me too," I said. "Now, here is the bad part: You don't earn leadership capital at the same rate as you spend it. In other words, for every dollar of leadership capital you earn, it is only worth about ten cents when you go to spend it. And to make matters even worse, the more you spend, the less your leadership capital is worth." Jane shook her head, letting me know I was losing her.

"Okay," I said. "Let's keep it simple. Rule number two (of the Five Rules) is, managers need to be on time, right?" Jane nodded. "Let's say we have a manager that is on time for an entire year. She is never late and she never leaves early can we agree that manager has earned a lot of leadership capital?" Nod.

"Now, for arguments sake, let's say that manager has some car trouble one day, and for the first time ever, she is late because of it. Will anyone give her a hard time about it?"

"No," Jane said. "Of course not, especially if she hasn't been late for an entire year."

"Exactly!" I said, getting up from the desk. "Because she has earned a ton of leadership capital by not being late for an entire year. It doesn't mean that everyone was okay with it and has forgiven her for being late. It means that she had earned more than enough leadership capital to pay for it. See?"

"Absolutely," Jane said.

"Good. Good," I said. "Now let's say her car trouble continues and she is late again the next day. No big deal, right?" Jane nodded. "What about the next day?" Nod. "And the next?" Nod.

"How many days can she be late before everyone begins to question her ability to be a manager?"

Jane Shrugged. "Not very many," she said.

"Not very many," I repeated. "In fact, if it is much more than a couple of days, or at most a week, people are going to start talking." Jane continued to nod and purse her lips. "Imagine that. A manager is on time every day for a year. She's never late and she never leaves early, yet you agree, with all that 'leadership capital' she's built up (or earned), when she goes to cash it in, it is only worth a couple of days, maybe a week."

"That sucks," Jane said.

"Agreed," I said. "How well do you remember the game?"

"Monopoly?" I nodded. "I played it all the time when I was a kid," she said.

"Good. Me too," I said. "Then you know, of all the properties that are for sale, the least expensive ones are right at the beginning of the game. They are Baltic Avenue and Mediterranean Avenue, which go for $60 each. The most expensive properties on the board are..."

"Boardwalk and Park Place," Jane said with a smile.

"Right," I said. "Boardwalk is $400 and Park Place is $350; they are the most sought after two pieces of property in the whole game and they are at the end. My question to you is, why?"

Jane didn't hesitate.

"Because if anyone lands on them, the rent is so high they won't be able to afford it and they will lose the game."

"Damn it Jane," I said pumping my fists into the air like I was fighting off a bee. To say I was excited, would have been an understatement.

"Okay. It also means that the person who owns Boardwalk and Park Place is likely to win the game, right?"

"Right."

"Okay," I said again, taking a deep breath. "Here it is, for all the tea in China, Jane. Are you ready?" Jane laughed and nodded.

"Here is the lesson: People who are new to the game of Monopoly will spend their money as fast as they get it. Whatever they land on first, they buy. Soon, after only a few rolls of the dice, they will be completely out of money."

"True," Jane said.

"Now, I don't know how long it has been since you played with someone new, or since you played with a couple of young kids, but as soon as they are out of money, they all start wanting to do the same thing: They negotiate. They are willing to do anything for more money." Jane's eyes got big and she started nodding.

"Wow," Jane said leaning back into her chair.

"If they had any experience with the game at all, they would have known better. They would have known that it is a far better strategy to be patient. To pass GO a few times and put some money in the bank before they start spending it on every roll of the dice. Instead, because they are new and excited, it doesn't take them long before they are completely out of money and out of the game.

"It is the same thing in management. A new manager with very little experience and leadership capital will spend it as fast as they get it. They will come in late, leave early, take thirty breaks a day and are never around when their staff needs them.

"As a result, their staff doesn't trust them or listen to them, and before you know it, the manager starts doing the only thing they can think of to remain being the manager; they start negotiating with their staff. They will let them come in late, leave early, and, of course, the manager will start doing all kinds of things their staff are supposed to be doing.

"When I ask why, they all tell me the same thing: 'I was always taught that you should never ask anyone to do anything you wouldn't do.' However, the truth is, they are out of leadership capital and they don't know of any other way to earn it." Jane rubbed her eyes with both hands and then pulled her hair back and sat like that, looking off into space with her hands resting on top of her head.

"Of course, by then, it is usually too late," I said.

"Wow," she said again. "Wow." I smiled.

"I know," I said. "Being good at managing is like trying to win a game of Monopoly. It takes patience and strategy, and more than anything else, it requires you to continually pass GO as many times as possible and when you do have to spend money (leadership capital) do it wisely." Jane continued to smile and nod.

"Wow," she said again. "Just, wow."

CHAPTER 16

GOLDEN RULE #3
CHOOSING YOUR BATTLES

"Sometimes you have to choose your friggin' battles," Mike said shaking his head with a half-smile. He watched me closely, hoping I agreed with him. I nodded and laughed.

"Sure," I said. "As long as you are okay with losing the battle." He laughed, then paused as he thought about what I said; which made me laugh.

"Ralph, I can't fight every single battle," he said, shaking his head. "If I did, I'd never get anything done around here."

"Ha!" I snorted. "I'm not so sure that's true," I said. "But I understand what you mean."

Several years ago, a friend of mine bought me a book called: Don't Sweat the Small Stuff, by Richard Carlson (Hyperion, 1996). As an aside to the main title, the author added a small subtitle that read: "and it's all small stuff." As if to say that we shouldn't sweat anything.

My friend said his wife had bought him a copy of the same book a year earlier. Just after he was promoted to a management position for the first time. She said she thought it would help him focus on what is important. He thought it did.

He said that when he read it, he thought of me. I didn't know if that was a compliment or not, so I just thanked him for thinking of me and took the book; but I never read it. The title alone was enough for me to know that it wasn't for me. I've been managing for way too long and I know better.

If you are one of those people that believe all the hype about not sweating the small stuff or that choosing your battles is the best way to be in charge, it is not your fault. This piece of sage advice is as common in management as the phrase "Break a leg" is in theater. Of course, in theater, they are being ironical. In management, they're not.

However, this concept of not "sweating the small stuff" or "choosing your battles" in management, will, if you are not careful bite you in the butt. And I'm not talking about a small bite that will feel better with a little rub and some aspirin. No. No. I'm talking about the kind of bite that will make you spin around, loose your balance and fall headfirst off that pedestal you manage from.

The first time I realized how counterproductive this practice of choosing your battles was, I was being written up for how poorly my team was doing. I was fairly new at managing and my District Manager, trying to be helpful while writing me up, asked me to go through all the job routines to see if there was something I was missing or misunderstanding about what everyone was supposed to be doing. I wasn't. I knew all the job routines like the back of my hand.

He looked at time and attendance records to see if people were coming in late or leaving early; they weren't. He looked at project calendars and schedules and talked ad nauseam about each one. However, it wasn't until we started walking around that he found the problem; it was me.

Without even realizing it, I was letting people get away with all kinds of little things that made it nearly impossible for them to get their jobs done. I let people take longer breaks, cut corners, move from one project to another without finishing any of them and on and on.

When he asked me why, I said, "I thought you were supposed to choose your battles." I remember him shaking his head and laughing.

"Who the hell told you that," he said. I shrugged, and with a smile I admitted.

"I didn't know."

Ever since that conversation, and write up, I have learned a lot about what can happen when managers don't sweat the small stuff, or when they choose their battles, and it is not good and can have dangerous consequences.

Consider this: One of the most iconic rock and roll bands of the 1980's, Van Halen, spent most of the 80's touring all over the world. As part of their contract, they had one very specific stipulation: they didn't want any brown M&M's.

Tucked in the pages and pages of legal jargon, logistical specifications and accommodation requests, Van Halen put in their contract, that they wanted a bowl of candy M&M's in their dressing room. However, in big capital letters they wrote: "WARNING: ABSOLUTELY NO BROWN ONES." And they were serious. The contract further stated, if they found any brown M&M's in the bowl of candy, the concert venue would forfeit their entire fee.

To an outsider, this might sound like an odd request, or worse, as an example of how unreasonable bands could be, just because they were famous. This was not, however, the case with Van Halen.

At the time, Van Halen was touring with a very large, state of the art and dangerous light show. Therefore, it was extremely important that the venue's production team followed the safety and logistical guidelines in the contract. To ensure they read the entire contract, the band added the brown M&M clause. That way, all the band had to do was go into their dressing room, grab the bowl of candy M&M's and be able to see right away–if the management team, had in fact, read the entire contract.

Van Halen knew, if the production's management team did not "sweat the small stuff," or they were the type who "chose their battles," they would likely miss some very large stuff which could result in a dangerous situation for both the band and their fans.

In the end, most managers who "choose their battles," usually do so for two reasons. Some managers choose their battles based on the size of the issue. They tend to believe in the notion that it is best not to "sweat the small stuff." They think some issues are too small to cause big problems. They are wrong. Small things can build up over time, and when they do, all kinds of unintended and sometimes really bad things, can happen.

Other managers choose their battles based on whether or not they think they can win. In this instance, if a manager doesn't think they can win the battle, then they won't see any reason to fight it. In fact, they will go out of their way to avoid it. This too is a problem. While there is some truth in the statement, "You can't win every battle." The point of choosing to fight a battle in management, is not to win, but to fight.

CHAPTER 17

You Won't Win Them All

One of my favorite words to throw around when talking about management is the word dichotomy. Simply put, a dichotomy is when an idea or a situation can be looked at or handled in ways that seem to contradict each other.

In management, a dichotomy is always present. That is to say, there is always more than one way to handle a situation, correct a problem or talk to an employee. The challenge, or dichotomy, is that some of these ways contradict each other.

Hence, the dichotomy of choosing your battles.

On one hand, fighting battles that you know you can't win seems counterproductive and a huge waste of time. Worse, some people believe fighting battles you know you can't win will cost you valuable leadership capital.

While I understand the sentiment; that it seems like a waste of time and perhaps counterproductive to fight battles you know you can't win. The dichotomy is, to be good at managing, you don't have to win, but you do have to fight.

Fighting, however, is not the right word. I am not suggesting that, in order to be a good manager, you have to get into a physical or even a verbal altercation with your employees. I am suggesting that, to be good at managing or, to put it another way, to be an effective manager, you will always have to speak up, even when you know speaking up isn't going to make an immediate difference.

Take call outs, as an example. A call out, sometimes called a "call off" or a "call in," is when an employee notifies their employer that they are not able to show up for work, despite being scheduled. The majority of call outs are due to the employee being sick. However, there are also transportation issues, childcare issues and other personal issues that are often cited for reasons an employee cannot make it to work.

Most employers have a policy regarding how and when an employee needs to contact their manager when calling out. Usually, this requirement stipulates the employee must call out at least two-hours prior to their scheduled start time. This requirement is designed to give the manager enough time to make adjustments for their absence.

Managers who are on the receiving end of these calls know how frustrating and difficult it can be to try to cover or replace someone with very short notice. However, most managers also know that, once an employee has called out, it is unlikely that they are going to change their mind and decide to come to work; even if the manager were to call and ask them to. Therefore, most managers will not follow up with the employee who has called out.

They know they cannot win the battle, (i.e. prevent the call out) so they have decided not to fight. The dichotomy, I would argue, is that by choosing not to fight or follow up with the employee, makes calling out permissible and extremely easy. And when you make calling out permissible and extremely easy, you get a lot of call outs.

To reiterate the point I made earlier, that this book was written for my managers initially, let me share with you our policy regarding call outs:

First, for the employee: (note this is not our complete policy, just an excerpt)

1. Employees are required to notify their manager at least two hours prior to the beginning of their shift if they are unable to make it to work.

2. Employees may choose to leave a voice message or a text message when calling out. However, it is up the employee to make sure their manager has received their message (this can be done by establishing direct person to person contact, via phone or by getting a text message response from the manager).

Next, for managers:

1. Managers are not allowed to accept call outs from any staff member for any reason, until the speak directly with the employee.
2. Managers must make an effort to contact every employee who calls out and find out why they have called out and what, if anything, we can do to help them get to work as soon as possible.
3. Managers are to reiterate how important the staff member is to the team and how their absence is going to affect both their teammates and customers.
4. Managers are to review the employee's schedule, ensuring they are able to return to work on their next scheduled day.
5. Managers are to track all call outs and share the ongoing results and consequences, if any are warranted, with the employee.

As you can see, our policy is to choose to fight or push back against all callouts. This does not mean that employees suddenly feel better, apologize for calling in, and rush in to work. That is not the point.

Our intention is to make calling out as difficult as possible for our employees. We want calling out to be the opposite of easy.

Of course, we don't do it in a negative way. In fact, we put the onus of contact on both the employee and the manager. Both are required to reach out to the other. They are required to communicate. Our managers are simply required to communicate more.

In the end, while choosing to fight battles you know you cannot win, may seem counterproductive in the short term, keep in mind that every time you don't speak up, you are setting a precedent that could last a very long time. Hence the dichotomy of management.

CHAPTER 18

COUNTER POINT: TACTICALLY PATIENT VS. CHOOSING YOUR BATTLES

Unlike the concept of "choosing your battles," where managers pick and choose which battle they are going to fight, being tactically patient is choosing how, and more importantly, when to fight your battles; not if.

Consider this: The last time I was fired, a guy I didn't know met me at the front door of my office building as I was coming back from lunch.

"Ralph?" he asked, extending his hand as I walked up to the building. I remember smiling, putting my hand out and nodding. He took it and told me he was from HR and wanted to know if I had a minute to talk. I did. I followed him to a small conference room, just inside the main corridor where he introduced me to someone else from HR; a woman. After a few pleasantries and sitting down he said, "We are going to make today your last day."

I took in a deep breath, ready to protest, when the woman slid a box across the table toward me.

"All of the stuff from your office is in here," she said. I exhaled slowly and sat back in my chair. Then I started crying.

Ha! I kid. I didn't start crying. How dare you... In fact, I did the opposite. I was so impressed by the way they were firing me, I told them as much. Using the turn of phrase: "We are going to make today your last day," is genius and disarming; I have been using it ever since. Then, if you think about the logistics they had to go through to pull this off right after lunch... it was all very impressive.

"We do everything we can to be as non-confrontational as possible," the guy said.

"Well done," I said and nodded. They went on to explain the reason for my termination and what my options were, but all I kept thinking about was the step by step process they used to get me into this room in order to have this conversation.

For those of you who have never had to let someone go, there is a lot to think about. How is the person likely to respond to the news they are being let go? Are they going to be upset? Are they going to be loud? Aggressive? Are they going to slam things? Who is going to be the one to talk to them and let them know they are, indeed, being let go? Is it going to be their direct manager, or someone from HR? Should there be witnesses? If so, who is going to be the witness? Should we let them go back to their desks or work stations to get their belongings, or should we have them all packed up beforehand. If so, who is doing the packing and when?

Finally, when should you let someone go? Should you talk to them right when they get to work, or should you wait until the end of the day? Should you wait until Friday?

A tactically patient manager looks for the right time to speak up, make a change, or address an issue. They do not choose which battles to fight, they choose when to fight; but they fight all battles. Knowing the difference is key to being a good manager.

CHAPTER 19

Golden Rule #4
Micro-The Four-Letter Word of Management

Eight-thousand, nine-hundred and seventy-two; that is how many nickels I would have if I received a nickel from every manager that ever said, "I shouldn't have to..."

- "I shouldn't have to check up on her all the time..."
- "I shouldn't have to constantly be showing him what to do..."
- "I shouldn't have to explain it to them every, single, time..."

- "I shouldn't have to call her every day to make sure she looked at the schedule..."
- "I shouldn't have to wonder who is showing up every day..."
- "I shouldn't have to, this... and I shouldn't have too, that..."

The truth is, if you want to be a good manager, you will have to be a micro-manager. Micro-managing is a necessary management tool that needs to be employed. Who you have to micro-manage and how often, is unfortunately not up to you; it is up to them. Some employees will need more, others will need less, all of them will need some.

Most employees who say they do not want to be micro-managed, simply mean that they do not want anyone checking up on their work because they don't want to be held accountable.

I am speaking from experience. I have been the type of employee who, if I didn't think you were going to check on my work I wouldn't do it. Or, if I did do it, I wouldn't have done it well. After a while (and it doesn't take long), if I didn't think you cared enough to check, then I too, wouldn't care.

In fact, there are still times when I get too busy or don't think I need to check up on someone only to find out that the task they said they completed, wasn't completed. When I ask them why they lied to me, they usually fall silent, not sure what to say, but I do.

"It's because you didn't think I was going to look," I say, a knowing smile on my lips. They nod slowly, reluctantly, and then seeing my smile, they smile.

"You got me," they say. "You got me."

It's not hard to understand why employees do this. Can you imagine working your butt off trying to make sure you're doing the best job possible only to have it go unnoticed? Can you imagine if even your manager didn't care enough to check in with you, to see what you have been up to? I have and it sucks.

On the other hand, if I knew my manager was going to check on my work, not only would I have it all done, but I would have done a really great job. In this sense, micro-managing isn't bad; it's magic.

It isn't just employees either; I know a lot of managers who say they do not want to be micro-managers. In fact, they believe the word "micro" is the four-letter word of management. However, and again I am talking from experience here, what managers are really saying isn't, "I shouldn't have to..." They are saying, "I don't want to..."

- "I don't want to check up on her all the time..."
- "I don't want to constantly be showing him what to do..."
- "I don't want to explain it to them every single time..."
- "I don't want to make sure she knows her schedule..."
- "I don't want to make sure I know who is showing up every day..."

In essence, what they are saying is: "I don't want to be a good manager."

When I was new to management, I too believed micro-managing was bad. That all it showed was a lack of trust in your employees. In a bizarre twist of reality, that only a lazy manager like me could come up with, I believed that good workers didn't need or want to be micro-managed. And so, in a weird way, I thought I was helping my employees become better workers by not checking in on them. Can you imagine the results I was getting?

I'll give you a hint, they were not good; they were bad.

Checking in, overseeing and making sure your staff are doing what they are supposed to be doing, when they are supposed to be doing it, is the job of the manager. The number of times you have to check in on them, or the number of times you have to explain things to them, is not up to you; it is up to them.

Managers who believe, "they shouldn't have too," or "micromanaging is bad" cost their companies millions and millions of dollars in lost productivity. Worse, this attitude often results in defective products, mishandled and broken equipment, attitudes, lawsuits, disgruntled employees, fist fights, arguments, high attrition rates and loss of customers.

Imagine being a customer to one of these managers and having to rely on them to produce a product or service for you. I am sure you, like me, have had an instance where you ordered something that was supposed to take one week to get to you and it took four.

Or you ordered one thing and they sent you something completely different.

When it is someone's birthday present that is late, or flowers that are not delivered on the right day, it sucks. However, when it is life-saving medical equipment or medication, and the company that supplies those products or services have managers that believe they "shouldn't have to be a micro-manager," it is more than just inconvenient, it is dangerous and often times has dire consequences.

CHAPTER 20

Golden Rule #5
Treat People the Way You Want to Be Treated

I live in a glass house. I moved in more than thirty years ago, though at the time I didn't know it. I didn't know that when you become a manager, in a sense, you are agreeing to move into a glass house. A house where everyone can see everything you do.

In my defense, I was young and naive and thought, like everyone else, as soon as I left work for the day, I could do anything I wanted. What I didn't know is that when you live in a glass house, everything you do, day or night, can be seen by anyone who cares to look; and unfortunately for me, a lot of people were looking, and still do. This, in essence, is the plight of management: People are always watching your every move.

Although it took me a long time to realize it, moving into a glass house has been one of the best things that has ever happened to me. Indeed, I am a better person and manager, because I learned a long time ago that everyone is aways watching me. This brings me to the 5th and final Golden Rule, which says that, to be good at managing, you should treat people the way you want to be treated.

For a long time, like all of the Golden Rules, I believed the hype. I thought treating people the way I wanted to be treated, was not only the right thing to do, especially since everyone was watching my every move, but then, everyone would treat me the same way. Then, I was punched in the throat by a 90lb housekeeper.

In fact, I wasn't just punched, I have been threatened, spit on, called names and have been the subject of more rumors and lies than I can count. All of this while trying my best to treat people the way I wanted to be treated; with dignity and respect. I didn't want to be threatened, or punched or spit on, or lied about, so I didn't do these things to anyone else. But it didn't matter. Some people are not going to treat you the same way that you treat them, no matter what you do.

Of all the things I have ever contemplated in management, the question of why we need managers in the first place, is not one that I have spent a lot of time thinking about, until now. Aside from the obvious, of helping people overcome obstacles and providing education, oversight, and support to employees, there is one aspect of management that I have overlooked for a long time.

A manager's job is to deal with difficult people.

The good news is that most people are decent, upstanding human beings who treat each other, even their managers, with a great deal of respect. Heck, most people give me respect before I am ever able to extend the same courtesy to them. However, there are some employees that are not good. There are some employees whose only intention is to cause chaos and mayhem. They look for fights, they lie, cheat, and steal. They do anything and everything they want, regardless of how it affects other people.

In these cases, I have learned that there are times when treating people the way I want to be treated doesn't work. Instead, I have to treat people the way they need to be treated.

This isn't only the case when I am dealing with an unruly or aggressive employee. There are times when I have to treat an employee with a lot more grace and patience than I would ever need.

In life, regardless of whether you are at work or at home, or if you are an hourly employee or the top CEO of an organization, living by the Golden Rule of treating people the way you want to be treated is solid advice. However, if you want to be good at managing people, you need to know how people need to be treated, and you need to treat them that way, even if it isn't the way you want to be treated.

CHAPTER 21

COUNTER POINT:
IT'S A LOT HARDER THAN IT LOOKS

have to go back to when I was eleven or twelve years old, to remember when I first started to understand the concept of working. We lived in a duplex in a rundown part of town. A place where we had plenty of cockroaches, but very little money. Both my parents worked at a state-run hospital for the mentally handicapped, and they hated it.

We had a neighbor named Kenny and he worked there too. He

and my dad would sit on the front stoop of our house and drink beer after work and complain, mostly about their managers.

My dad was a loud talker, so it didn't matter where you were. You could be inside the house trying to watch television or in the backyard playing football, and you could still hear him. There were times when, and I am not making this up, I would be at my friend John's house, which was a couple of houses down, and we could still hear my dad complaining about his job.

I'm fairly certain this is where I first started learning about the "Golden Rules" of management, through osmosis. Of course, my dad, having never been in a management position, believed the golden rules were like the Ten Commandments. As if they were passed down by God himself, and any manager that didn't follow them had no right to be in a management position.

It is no wonder, in retrospect, why I was always so willing to buy into and follow the "Golden Rules" of management, even though I knew intuitively that following them made me an ineffective manager; I was raised to believe they were true and, probably more importantly, I wanted to please my dad.

Plus, in my defense, the Golden Rules make management sound easy. Imagine if all you had to do to be a good manager was praise employees publicly and reprimand them privately; or walk around picking up random pieces of trash off the floor so that everyone knew that you didn't think you were better than them. Imagine if all you had to do was tell your employees what they are supposed to do, one time, and then never have to check up on them ever again. Imagine if you could just walk around handing out high fives and compliments, because high fives and compliments are what you would want if you were the employee. It sounds awesome, doesn't it? Heck, it sounds easy.

Management, however, is not easy.

Management is going to require more hours, more work, and more attention than most people think it is. A lot of people believe that getting promoted to a management position is like winning the lottery. They think life is going to be easier now, with less work and more time to do it in. These people are always the first to go.

Throughout this book, I keep pointing at one thing or another as the "one mistake" everyone makes, as if one mistake has a way of overshadowing them all. The truth is, most mistakes on their own, typically are not detrimental to your success. The problem is, most of these mistakes have a compounding effect. Meaning that, the more mistakes you make, the harder it is for you to recover from.

Therefore, it is my hope that, if you take anything away from this book, it is this: Being a good manager requires hard work; and hard work can overcome just about any management mistake. You can break all of the rules of management, and follow every Golden Rule, despite their ability to undermine you, and you can still be very successful. All you have to do is work harder than the mistakes you make.

CHAPTER 22

Don't Be Evil

Something bad happened the first time I became a manager. I became unreasonable. I was bull-headed, inflexible, authoritative, and mean. In essence, I became a tyrant. I didn't mean to. In fact, I was just as shocked as everyone else was.

It is a profound and powerful feeling, being put in charge. In fact, the feeling of power began to take shape the day my boss pulled me aside and asked if I would be interested in taking on more responsibility. Almost immediately, my head began to swell, my back stiffened, and I began to day dream and fantasize, playing out tiny little scenarios in my head.

I was going to be the best boss ever. I was going to be both helpful and fun, while at the same time being firm and fair. If I saw anyone slacking off or not doing the right thing, I was going to speak up and people would listen to me.

I was sixteen years old when it happened. I was put in charge for the first time. One of my first acts as a manager was to get Randy, a guy two years older than me, to put some tools away. He refused, telling me to do it myself. I challenged him, asking him if he knew who he was talking to. He laughed as if it didn't matter· as if I didn't matter. Then he threw a tape measure at me. Without thinking, I reacted poorly. I punched him in the face. He backed up, stunned. Then he rushed me. Soon we were on the ground, throwing fists and elbows. That is when my boss showed up and fired me on the spot.

My first time as a manager lasted a total of eight minutes, but it was too late. I had tasted what it was like to be in charge, and I was hooked.

I didn't know it at the time, but my origin story, from beginning to end, from the time my boss asked me to be in charge to the time my boss fired me for not being very good at it, was common. In fact, as it turns out, going from a well-intended, hard-working individual, to a power-hungry tyrant is more than just common, it is easier than you'd think.

One of the first psychologists to study and prove this phenomenon was a psychology professor from Stanford University, Philip

Zimbardo. In 1971, he conducted the now-infamous, Stanford Prison Experiment.

The experiment was made up of male college students who volunteered to spend fourteen days in a makeshift prison in the basement of the psychology department. The roles each would play, that of a prison guard or a prisoner, was determined by a simple flip of a coin.

Within twenty-four hours, the prisoners had started to push back against the authority of the prison guards. The prison guards, trying to maintain a semblance of both order and authority, began to do anything and everything to subdue their prisoners.

They used fire extinguishers. They put prisoners in solitary confinement and took away as many privileges as they could. They started with their mattress pads, forcing them to sleep on a concrete floor, to get them in line. When that didn't work, they stripped them of their clothes and became more and more abusive as the days went on.

Six days later, the experiment was cancelled: eight days early.

In conclusion, Philip Zimbardo stated that the study illustrated something called the cognitive dissonance theory (Festinger, Leon: 1957); which occurs when a person acts in a way that is contrary to their beliefs or values when placed in a stressful situation.

In layman's terms, what the Stanford Prison Experiment showed, was this: Being in a management position is stressful, and stress can cause even the most well-intended of us to act in a way that we would have never believed possible. That is, evil.

However, while this experiment and subsequent conclusions may make sense; it is important to understand that the real problem is not a manager's propensity to act evil. The real problem is, being an evil manager doesn't work.

CHAPTER 23

BEING EVIL DOESN'T WORK

One of the biggest challenges I have had to overcome, as a manager, is my proclivity to be default aggressive. I have a type "A" personality. I talk loud. I walk fast. I have no patience for nonsense, and I rarely let the little things go.

As a result, I've had a reputation of being rough around the edges. As someone who rules with an iron fist. I have been called unreasonable, hot-headed, and mean. I have even been called a bully.

For a long time, I have worn these notions as a badge of honor. I liked having the reputation of being tough. I like people knowing that I have high expectations and I like having high standards.

However, I have also taken things too far and I have learned, the hard way, that when you take things too far, it doesn't work.

In 1961, a Yale University psychologist, a guy named Stanley Milgram, was the first person to prove that, "being evil doesn't work" when he conducted what is now known as the Milgram experiment.

To do this, he asked volunteers to help a researcher conduct a study on the effects of punishment, or in this case painful shocks, on a person's ability to memorize and learn.

The set up was simple. A volunteer was placed in a room with the researcher. In a separate room, adjacent to the one they were in, another person was hooked up to a machine. The researcher would ask the person in the other room a series of questions. If they got the answer wrong, they would ask the volunteer to press a button which would give them an electrical shock. The more questions the person got wrong, the more intense the shock became.

The dial on the machine that registered the power of the shock, went from zero volts, to a max of 400 volts. Or, to put it another way, it went from barely being felt, to extremely painful.

The key to this experiment is that the volunteers were told they were conducting the research on the person on the other side of the wall; the person who was answering the questions. However, the person on the other side of the wall was an actor, there were no actual electrical shocks and the person they were really studying, was the volunteer.

What the researcher was really trying to find out, was how far the volunteer would go, shocking the person on the other side of the wall, just because they were told to. Keep in mind, every time the person got a question wrong, the researcher asked the volunteer to turn up the voltage on the machine and push the button.

The actor would then scream, cry, and beg the volunteer to stop. Sometimes, they would complain that their heart was hurting or their head, or that some part of their body had gone numb. Other times they would simply stop responding, as if they had passed out from the pain. Each time, the researcher would ask the volunteer to continue to push the button, sending as much as 400 volts of electricity to the person on the other side of the wall. As a result, a whopping 60% of the time, the volunteer did.

At the end of the experiment, the initial conclusion was that ordinary people had an unusual proclivity to fall into a subservient role and follow the orders of an authority figure, even if they knew that by doing so, they were hurting someone else.

However, a recent examination of that study has revealed something that has been overlooked the entire time.

As you can imagine, asking a volunteer to repeatedly shock someone, with increasingly higher and higher volts of electricity, just because they were getting questions wrong, was not an easy task. In fact, the researcher had to put pressure on all of the volunteers to get them to continue to press the button.

To do this, the researcher countered each protest with the following requests: "Please administer the shock," they'd say. Or, "You must administer the shock." Or, "The experiment requires you to administer the shock."

Finally, if none of those worked, the researcher would demand the volunteer press the button saying, "You have no choice but to follow my instructions and administer the shock."

It turns out, the most effective turn of phrase the researcher used to get the volunteers to keep pressing the button and shock the person on the other side of the wall, was the first one: "Please administer the shock." This turn of phrase worked 70% of the time.

In stark contrast, when the researcher used the last turn of phrase: "You have no choice but to follow my instructions…" it didn't work at all. In fact, it had the opposite effect. Rather than siding with the authority figure (the researcher), and buying into the importance of the experiment, the volunteer took pity on the person on the other side of the wall.

Up until this point, the volunteers believed the researcher was conducting the experiment for the sake of science. However, once the researcher started to demand the volunteer continue, even though the person on the other side of the wall was begging them not to, the researcher, and the experiment began to look more sadistic than it did scientific.

Therefore, the original conclusion, that ordinary people had an unusual proclivity to be evil, or to follow those that are deemed evil, is false. In reality, the more demanding, unreasonable, and mean a manager is, the less effective they become.

In the end, being evil doesn't work.

CHAPTER 24

FALL SEVEN, RISE EIGHT

The opening scene is a classic. It is Thanksgiving Day in 1973. Lucy, always the antagonist, convinces Charlie Brown to try to kick a football. If you are a fan of the Peanuts cartoon, you know exactly what is about to happen. Because it always happens.

Charlie Brown knows it too, but like he has in the past, he hopes this time it is going to be different. He hopes Lucy is going to be different. He hopes she will do what she says she is going to do and hold the ball steady.

"This year, I am really going to kick that football," Charlie Brown says getting ready.

Then, throwing caution and reason to the wind, he runs forward with his head down and his spirits up. In his mind he is envisioning a solid kick; one for all the ages. The ball is going to soar so high into the air that everyone will see it. Charlie Brown, for once in his life is going to be a hero.

Lucy, however, does what Lucy always does... She pulls a fast one and at the very last second, she rips the ball away. Charlie Brown can't react in time and rather than connecting with the ball, his feet fly straight up into the air and he lands with a thud. A look of bewilderment covers his face.

The following year, Charlie Brown will try again. And again, Lucy will do what Lucy does. She will pull the ball away just as Charlie Brown tries to kick it. Not deterred, Charlie Brown will try again, and again, and again.

One of the biggest challenges in management is that it is full of "Lucy's." People who convince you that they are going to be helpful. That you can trust them. That they will do what they are supposed to be doing. Then, just when you need them the most, they'll yank the ball away and laugh as you tumble head over heels.

Suddenly, like Charlie Brown, instead of looking like a hero, you feel like a zero.

For many managers, especially those that are new to the field, this Charlie Brown experience is enough for them to question why they ever decided to raise their hand in the first place.

The truth is, failing in management is hard. Probably harder than failing in any other position, due to its public nature. However, and I know this might sound odd, failing in management is the best thing that can happen to you; as long as you don't give up.

The Japanese have a phrase: Nanakorobi, yaoki which means, "the only way to overcome failure is to rise above it." The literal English translation is: "Fall seven, rise eight."

As I stated in the beginning of this book, there is a shortage of people who are willing to raise their hand and say, "Pick me." That is, there is a shortage of people who are willing to be in charge. That is why it doesn't matter what industry you are in, your ethnicity, background, gender, education and sometimes even your experience level; if you are willing to fall down seven times and rise up eight, you can be a good manager, and the truth is, we need you.

CHAPTER 25

BEING GREAT IS OVERRATED

After Rocky Balboa defeated Apollo Creed to become the Heavyweight Champion of the World, in the movie Rocky II (United Artist, 1979), he spent the next three years defending his title against anyone and everyone who challenged him. Soon, Rocky became a huge celebrity and his face was everywhere: on candy bars, in television commercials and on magazine covers. To this day, one of the most famous depictions of Rocky is a huge bronze statue that sits in front of the famed Philadelphia Museum of Art.

If you haven't seen the iconic movie series known as Rocky, it is worth watching. It is about a down and out boxer who is given the chance of a lifetime to fight the heavyweight champion of the world and he actually wins. It is one of the greatest underdog movies of all time.

By the third movie (Rocky III), however, Rocky has bought into all of the hype and is now convinced that he is no longer an underdog. Indeed, he is now the greatest boxer of all time. That is, until he meets Clubber Lang, a fast-talking fighter with a huge chip on his shoulder and enough muscles to carry it. He knocks Rocky out in the second round.

The movie does a great job highlighting what happens to someone when they start to believe they are the greatest of all time; that is, they stop doing all of the things that made them great. In the movie, Rocky's manager, Mickey, a formidable boxer in his own time, summed it up nicely saying:

"Three years ago you were supernatural... But then, the worst thing happened to you, you got civilized."

It doesn't just happen in the movies; however, it happens to military fighter pilots too.

In a recent study of what the military calls, "aviation accidents," they have identified an unsettling statistic. New pilots, those who have been flying for less than two years, were more likely than not, to have an accident, (i.e. crash an airplane). In fact, having an aviation accident within the first two years of a pilot's career is so likely to happen that it is expected and, quite literally, budgeted for.

The good news is, around the two-year mark, the amount of aviation accidents drops to nearly zero. The reason for this is obvious. The more training and experience you have, the less likely you are going to make mistakes. However, this is not the unsettling statistic they found, that happens much later; four years later to be exact.

It turns out, although the military sees a dramatic drop in aviation accidents around the time a pilot reaches two years of service, they start seeing a huge increase of aviation accidents when that same pilot reaches their sixth year. At first, none of this made any sense. How can a new pilot go from having no experience and a lot of accidents to spending four years with little or no incidents, to then suddenly having more accidents?

It's easy... They started to buy into all the hype. After four years of accident-free flying, these pilots started to believe they were great. So great, in fact, they stop performing all of their safety checks. They start taking unnecessary risks. And they stop doing all the things that made them great in the first place. In the end, like Rocky, they got too overconfident.

This problem, of course, extends beyond the movies and fighter pilots; unfortunately, it happens to magicians and managers.

It never dawned on me to consider the trajectory of Marco the Magician's career. How, in a very few short years he went from packing school auditoriums; performing for thousands of scream-ing kids, to pretending to spill ketchup on an unsuspecting patron in a steak house and making salt disappear.

"He used to be really great," a friend of mine said when I started calling around trying to find out what had happened to him. "I think he just got old, or maybe he just got tired of performing for a bunch of screaming kids," he said.

"Maybe," I agreed. "But you weren't there. The first time I saw him perform, when I was in the sixth grade, he was amazing." I leaned back in my chair and took in a deep breath. I was holding the phone to my head, but I didn't say anything. I thought back to that day in the school auditorium when he picked me. "More than just amazing," I said finally. "He loved it. He really loved performing."

"That happens to all of us," my friend said.

"What happens?" I said.

"You know. Once you get really good at something, even if you love it, you stop trying so hard. Before you know it, you are no longer as good as you once were, and maybe performing card tricks at a restaurant is now the only thing he can do."

"Maybe," I said nodding along in thought. "Maybe."

Over the years, I have worked with, recruited, hired, and trained hundreds of managers. Every time I meet a brand new manager, I get excited. I can't wait to tell them everything I know. I want them to be so successful, I often overwhelm them with facts and figures and stories... tons and tons of stories.

However, when I meet a manager that has some experience, I'm skeptical. I'm reserved. I'm less interested in spewing facts and figures and more interested in trying to gage where they are in their career.

Are they confident enough to be good, or are they too confident and think they're great? Talk about a dichotomy. The fact that you can be too confident, or have too much experience doesn't seem right, but it is. In my experience, managers who think they are great, don't work as hard as those that are still trying to be.

In the end, being a good manager comes down to following a handful of rules, avoiding common mistakes and not being evil. Don't worry about being great; being great is more than just a cliche, it is overrated.

EPILOGUE

Now What?

In 1987, while putting the finishing touches on their debut album, Appetite for Destruction, the band Guns & Roses hovered over a large mixing board in a cramped recording studio in Burbank, C.A. For more than an hour, they sat there listening to one song: Sweet Child O' Mine, over and over again.

Their producer, Spencer Proffer thought the song was missing something. The musicians agreed. However, it didn't matter how many times they listened to the song, no one could come up with anything. Then, Axl Rose, the lead singer and writer of the song, began singing the question everyone was asking: "Where do we go… Where do we go now… Where do we go…" He repeated it over and over so many times that it became part of the song.

As fate would have it, repeating the question, "Where do we go," turned out to be exactly what the song needed. The song, and this lyrical breakdown at the end, became Guns & Roses third hit single and their only #1 song in the United States.

Now what…

I have been walking around with this book for weeks, reading and rereading every chapter and every word. For a while I thought I was finished. However, like the producer for Guns & Roses, the more I read the book, the more I realized something was missing.

In this book, I have gone through great lengths to explain the rules of management. I have given you plenty of warnings, and I have told you how most people fail. What I haven't done, however, is tell you how win. Or, for that matter, how to play the game. The game of management.

First of all, I would argue the best way to approach management is like a game. A game where the strategy is to win and by winning, I mean that you are able to get your employees to do their job. Keep in mind, you are not likely going to win every hand, or every day, for that matter. You are not always going to roll doubles, or get pocket aces. Sometimes you are going to be dealt a terrible hand and still be expected to win, or at the very least, not lose.

Games, like management, require more than just a basic under-standing of the rules. To win at any game requires skill, experience, and strategy. Below are a handful of strategies and tips that I have learned over the years, and, in the end, need to be part of this book.

Become an expert. One of the main reasons anyone is promoted into a leadership position is because of how good they are at their job. At the same time, I cannot tell you how many managers I meet who only know the job they had, prior to their promotion. If you want to win at the game of management, you have to become an expert at all the positions under your command.

Don't stop learning. The more you know about each position, the more credibility you will have with your team, and, more importantly, the more you will be able to assist and oversee.

Look for trouble. I can't stress this one enough. Every time I interact with any of my staff, I am always looking for things they are not doing correctly. I focus on the small stuff. I look at uniforms, headsets, footwear, and cell phones. I focus on timing: Where are they? Where should they be? Are they ahead of schedule or behind? I look at what they are doing: Is it right? Is it wrong? Should it be better? Is there something I could, or should be showing them? Is there something they could be showing me?

Correct things immediately. Being tactically patient (Ch. 18) is solid advice for a lot of big things that may develop into something bigger. However, there is something to be said about timing. The longer you wait to correct an issue, the harder it will be, for both you and the employee, to deal with.

Employees believe that, if you don't correct an issue right away, then whatever it was they were doing wasn't wrong. Even if they know it was wrong. If you see it and they know you saw it, and you still didn't do anything about it... then it becomes your fault, not theirs.

It sounds silly, I know. But that is how the game is played.

Don't act like a hammer. This is one of the hardest lessons for me and I didn't learn it on my own. A friend, knowing I needed help as a manager, bought me a copy of the book, The One Minute Manager by Ken Blanchard (Berkley Trade, 1986). This book changed my entire understanding of what it takes to be a good manager. As a matter of fact, this is one of the most important books on management that I have ever read, and it continues to be the number one book that I give out as a gift to new managers. I cannot recommend it enough.

That being said, before I read the book, I was the worst boss when it came to letting my employees know they messed up. I would bring it up over and over again; sometimes for days and days. I truly treated my employees like they were nails and I was a hammer. However, once I read the chapter titled: 'One Minute Reprimanding,' and learned how much more effective it was to reprimand someone quickly (less than a minute) and then let it go, I became a better manager.

Bonus: This simple concept of not hammering my employees for mistakes they made completely changed our team dynamics. Not only did my employees work hard not to repeat mistakes, but when they did make mistakes, they easily and quickly owned up to them. Imagine that. Suddenly, instead of having to look for mistakes, my employees were showing me theirs.

Apologize quickly and often. You are going to make mistakes. All of us do. In management, we are required to read and react to situations quickly. As a result, it is easy to make mistakes. However, the best thing a manager can do when they do make a mistake is apologize, quickly and often.

Brace for impact. It's all fun and games until someone gets hurt. Management can be a contact sport, both in the physical sense and metaphorically speaking. The worst part is, managers never see it coming. We always get blindsided on some random Tuesday. This job will test you and make you question your sanity. It isn't for the faint at heart. One of the best pieces of advice I have ever received was simply this: You better toughen up if you want to be a manager.

Everyone is lying. Okay, so maybe not everyone. However, from a strategic point of view, being skeptical is sound advice. Keep in mind, everyone is trying to win the game of management. Some are trying to win as a manager, and some are trying to beat the manager. To win, many are willing to bluff, cheat, steal, and lie; and some even get lucky.

You won't like them all. Finally, to get one of the most important strategic lessons on management, we have to listen to one of the greatest child educators; a woman by the name of Rita Pierson. In 2013, after teaching for more than 40 years, Mrs. Pierson was invited to give a TED talk summarizing everything she has learned in teaching.

Her talk was titled, "Every Kid Needs a Champion," (TED: Ideas Worth Spreading, May 3, 2013, www.ted.com/talks/rita_pierson_every_kid_needs_a_champion). One of the most impactful statements she makes when talking about how to be a successful teacher is, "You won't like all the kids, but they can never know." The same is true in management.

This brings me to my final strategic tip: Learn how to bluff or pretend. Good managers master the art of acting. There are days when we all don't feel like showing up, or working hard, or following up with our staff. There are times when you won't be dealt the best hand. However, if you want to win any game, no one can ever know.

ACKNOWLEDGEMENTS

If you are familiar with any of my previous books, or if you receive my weekly newsletter then you know that I write about real people. Real people, in real situations trying their best to manage in chaotic environments. This book is no different.

As such, it is important for me to acknowledge and thank all the managers that I have worked with over the years and especially my current management team. Your curiosity, hard work, and willingness to push back when you don't agree with me, makes all of us stronger, more effective and in the end, good managers.

To my best friends Adam Duke and Devan Luciano, two people

who are on the same path as me, that is, trying to be, and produce the best managers on the planet. Thank you both for always being there for me.

Finally, to my team, India Brown, Chad Sweeney and everyone at Four-Nineteen Press; your help continues to be instrumental in my success, and I appreciate each and every one of you.

One final thought: As a writer, teacher and acting manager, I am always researching articles, reading books, and listening to podcast to gain different perspectives and to learn. While many authors and podcasts host have greatly influenced me over the years, there are a few people that I want to publicly recognize, in the hopes that my readers will look them up, and become their readers.

Jocko Willink and Leif Babin, Peter Drucker, Jordan Peterson, Ken Blanchard, John Maxwell, Brian Tracy, and Jim Rohn, to name a few.

Do yourself a favor and look up the people on this list. Listen to their podcasts, read their books and when they have a profound effect on you, and trust me, they will... reach out and let them know.

Spread the Love

If you loved this book and found it useful, would you please consider leaving a review on Amazon. com or Barnesandnobbles.com or wherever you purchased or downloaded this book? The more reviews a book receives, the more exposure it gets, and as a result, the more people it reaches.

That is the goal of this book, to reach more people.

Thank you!

Cut Here

Cut Here

TRASH

Do you have what it takes to lead?

www.RalphPeterson.com

.

Made in USA - Kendallville, IN
1183748_9780998926865
10.22.2020 0810